Old Kilmarnock
Guthrie Hutton

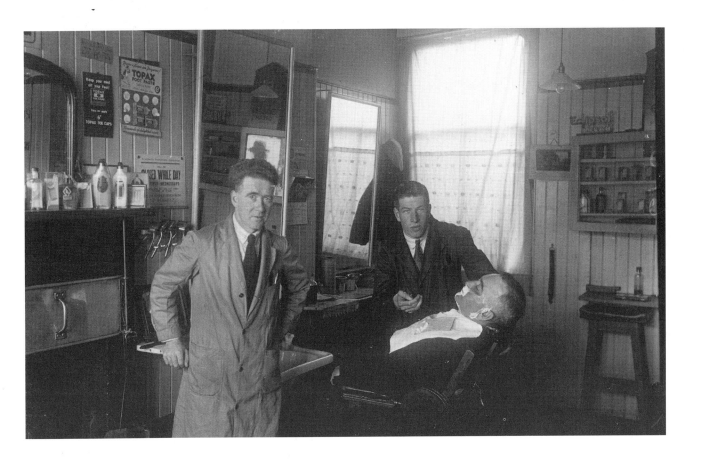

Photographed in 1936, this unidentified barber's shop has a sign on the wall indicating the Wednesday holiday supported by the Kilmarnock Shopkeepers' Association. Whole- and half-day holidays were once rigidly adhered to, but are now largely a thing of the past, as is having a hot shave with an open razor honed on a leather strop. This interior is typical of a traditional barber's: the men's dust coats and their practice of keeping razors, scissors and combs in their breast pockets provide a rare snapshot of a world superseded by salons and stylists.

ISBN 9781840334180

The often caricatured bonnet was essential headgear for the Scottish male. Bonnets were usually blue, although well-to-do and professional men tended to wear more expensive black ones. They were flat, round and knitted from wool using three needles to make them seamless. The knitters belonged to a small group of families who jealously guarded their rights to participate in the trade and controlled these rights through the town's Incorporation of Bonnetmakers and Dyers. That may have seen off local competition, but could do nothing to prevent neighbouring Stewarton claiming to be 'The Bonnet Town' – or its knitters winning a large nineteenth century military contract. Killie, however, was immortalised in song: 'Wi' ma big Kilmarnock bonnet as I ran to catch the train …'.

Acknowledgements

I am grateful to East Ayrshire Council's Arts and Museums for permission to use the pictures on the following pages: 18 (upper and lower), 31 (upper), 34 (upper and lower), 59 (upper), 62 (lower), 70 (upper and lower), 77 (upper and lower), 78 (lower) and 85 (lower). I must also thank the splendid Dick Institute, which provided the kind of obscure information needed to compile a book like this. I am grateful too to Diageo which supplied the Johnnie Walker pictures on pages 64 (upper and lower) and 65 (upper). The Mines Rescue picture on page 72 has been taken from my book *Mining: Ayrshire's Lost Industry*, and I must again thank John Borland, sadly this time posthumously, who lent it to me for that book. Stuart Marshall provided research material and pictures, mainly of the football club. Margaret Graham helped with pictures of performers and politicians, Jim Brown and David Warrillow supplied some useful pictures, and Amrit Singh helped with the story of Walker & Templeton. Tractor enthusiasts Pete Small, John Melloy and John Caldwell all helped with information and pictures of Massey-Harris. I must thank them all, and also bus enthusiast Robert Grieves for his considerable assistance.

Further Reading

'An Old Player', *Fifty Years of the Kilmarnock FC*, 1919

Beattie, Frank, *Greetings from Kilmarnock*, 1994

Beattie, Frank, *Streets and Neuks of Old Kilmarnock*, 2000

Beattie, Frank, *Proud Kilmarnock*, 2002

Brotchie, A.W. and Grieves, R.L., *Kilmarnock's Trams and Buses*, 1984

Close, R., *Ayrshire & Arran: an Illustrated Architectural Guide*, 1992

Donnachie, Bill, *Who's Who of Kilmarnock FC*, 1989

McKay, Archibald, *The History of Kilmarnock*, 5th (revised) edition, 1909

Mackay, James A., *Kilmarnock: a History of the Burgh of Kilmarnock and of Kilmarnock and Loudoun District*, 1992

Malkin, John, *Pictorial History of Kilmarnock*, 1989

Robertson, W., *Kilmarnock Equitable Co-operative Society: a Fifty Year Record*, 1910

Shaw, James Edward, *Ayrshire 1745– 1950*, 1953

Wear, Russell, *Barclay 150*, 1990

Introduction

Places beginning with 'Kil' are usually said to have been associated with an early Christian holy man, but there is scant evidence for a Saint Marnock and it has been suggested that the Kil should be read as Kyle. While Kilmarnock's origins are thus unclear, what is not in question is that over time a small town or village grew up beside the Kilmarnock Water. The river was the key. Its water provided one of life's essentials as well as power to drive a mill. Dean Castle, which protected the little town clustered around the kirk, was situated upstream at the confluence of two smaller tributaries.

For centuries the Boyd family, up at the castle, played its part in the jostling for power and prestige that counted for government in Scotland's turbulent past. Meanwhile, down in the crowded town, people just got on with their lives. In the seventeenth century they were caught up in the religious turmoil which followed the attempt by Charles I to impose an Episcopal form of worship on the Presbyterian Scots. People who opposed this by signing the National Covenant, first drawn up in 1638, became known as Covenanters, and had strong support in Ayrshire.

Hostility between Covenanters and the Crown grew increasingly bitter, and in 1666 the heads of two executed Ayrshire men were displayed in Kilmarnock as a warning to others. Troops led by the ruthless General Dalziel were based in and around the town, and for a time made life unpleasant for the people. Despite this, they failed to suppress support for the Covenanters. Men continued to fight for their beliefs, and in a final act of barbarism a man named John Nisbet was hanged at the Cross in 1683. A plaque, now in the Burns shopping mall, marks the spot.

Throughout this time people earned a living from crafts including weaving, making men's bonnets and ladies cowls, working metal, making cutlery, tanning and producing finished leatherwork. No doubt these activities would have continued to evolve, had the town's fortunes not been changed by the fateful decision of William Boyd, 4th Earl of Kilmarnock, to join Bonnie Prince Charlie's Jacobite Rebellion in 1745. After the Battle of Culloden he was captured, tried and executed, and the consequent loss of the family estates severed the bonds that tied the town to a powerful landowner. With no lordly brake on progress, Kilmarnock was able to let rip when the time came for industrial expansion.

The town had a brief moment in the spotlight in 1786 when the first edition of Robert Burns' poems was published by John Wilson. It sold out, but Wilson was unwilling to risk another run, and with the second printing done in Edinburgh that first 'Kilmarnock' edition has been elevated to an exalted status amongst lovers of Burns and books everywhere.

The town got a powerful landowner again when William Cavendish-Bentinck, Marquis of Titchfield, gained control of the estates through marriage (he inherited the title Duke of Portland later). The duke positively encouraged new ventures, developing the coal on his estate and building one of the first railways in Scotland to get it to the sea at Troon harbour. Later, in the 1840s, the combination of coal and railways further helped to transform the town when one of the main lines between Glasgow and England was opened up through Kilmarnock.

Ready access to fuel and transport gave business and commerce a strategic advantage, and a range of industries developed. Some of these, like textiles, carpet weaving and making shoes, grew out of earlier craft skills, but others were born of the new industrial age. These included precision engineering, fireclay products and building railway locomotives. It was a varied mix of activity and it brought a period of prosperity that lasted for over a hundred years.

When decline came after the mid-1960s it seemed to affect all of the town's industries at once. The diversity which at another time might have insulated Kilmarnock against trouble couldn't prevent the downturn. Some industry kept going in a reduced form, but the impact of all the closures and contractions had a devastating effect on the local economy.

It wasn't easy for people to come to terms with Kilmarnock's post-industrial reality, but the town is now shaking off the dust of decline as new uses are found for old factory sites. The next chapter in Kilmarnock's crowded history has already opened, and if the past is anything to go by it will be a lively story.

Dean Castle with a new roof in 1924.

It is likely that a church has existed at or near the site of the present Laigh (Low) Kirk since the thirteenth century. The kirk was always at the heart of the town, although the present structure was only erected in 1802 and replaced a building dating from about 1750. The need to build a new church arose in October 1801. As the congregation gathered for worship, some plaster fell from the ceiling causing panic. People rushed to get out while others were still trying to enter, and 29 were killed in the crush. The new church was given a number of exits to ensure that a similar tragedy could not occur again.

The Laigh Kirk is seen here about 1900 looking along Cheapside from the Cross, a place where people met to do business, or simply gathered for a blether before the inexorable growth of road traffic pushed such activity away.

Kilmarnock has been fighting a seemingly endless battle with road transport since the invention of the internal combustion engine, which is ironic for a railway town! Within 30 years of the picture on the facing page being taken, traffic control arrangements had significantly altered the way the Cross looked and worked. People had been pushed to the edges, and a points policeman stood on the spot formerly occupied by the statue of 'Jimmie' Shaw.

Twenty years on from the above picture and a horse and cart can still be seen at the Cross. Traffic volumes have increased to such an extent that a roundabout has replaced the policeman and fences have been erected to stop pedestrians going anywhere near the spot where they used to congregate. Before the end of the twentieth century a bypass road, the A77, had been built to keep through traffic away from the town, internal vehicle movements were routed round an endlessly circulating one-way system and the Cross had been paved and pedestrianised.

The area surrounding the Cross was once filled with a congested jumble of buildings connected by a warren of narrow lanes and closes. Some of these were cleared at the start of the nineteenth century to allow new streets with grand-sounding names to be driven through. Portland Street, seen here about 1900 before the introduction of trams, was one of these. It was created to make the road to and from Glasgow more direct, and replaced the somewhat tortuous route along Fore and High Streets.

In this view of Portland Street, taken about ten years after the picture above, two boys are crossing the road in front of a Riccarton-bound tram. One appears to be carrying on his head the kind of shallow wooden baker's tray used to convey unwrapped bread and rolls to customers – not perhaps the most hygienic way to transport food, but people were less aware of such concerns then and fresh local produce was tastier than today's mass production.

Standing in a box, which doubles as a road sign, a policeman directs a cyclist through the Cross and past Portland Street. The picture was taken on 4 July 1936, the same day as the temperance demonstration advertised on the banner slung across the street. The sunshine brought out the crowds to watch the parade, which wound round a circuit of streets and preceded the crowning of Jessie Currie as the town's third Temperance Queen at Howard Park's bandstand. The ceremony was performed by Margaret Robertson, Kilmarnock's previous queen and the Scottish Temperance Queen, an honour that had been bestowed on her the previous autumn.

Portland Street was one of the town's principal shopping streets, and one of its main shops was that of the Kilmarnock Equitable Co-operative Society. Formed in 1860, the society originated in a room in Princes Street, expanding to operate a number of branches around the town and county. In 1866 Portland Street became the site of its main shop, and a decade later another shop in the street was taken over. A new building made of red Ballochmyle stone (seen on the left of this 1948 view) was opened in 1905. The bays facing the street were decorated to represent industry and justice, two things of great importance to co-operators.

This picture was probably taken in 1904 at the time of the introduction of electric trams – or 'sparkies' as they were known locally. Kilmarnock's was not a large system. The principal route ran between the burgh boundaries at Riccarton and Beansburn, and a second line branched off at the Cross along London Road to Hurlford. This car at the junction of Portland and George Streets is bound for the 'Station', the terminus for trams from Hurlford, which was actually adjacent to the High United Free Church. The depot was situated at Riccarton Bridge next to the power station. Kilmarnock's tram system continually struggled to be profitable, and plans to extend the tracks to Bonnyton and Crosshouse were never implemented. The Hurlford route was discontinued in December 1924, and with losses mounting the decision was taken to cease operations on the main line. Before this could be implemented, the General Strike of May 1926 brought the service to a standstill and it never restarted.

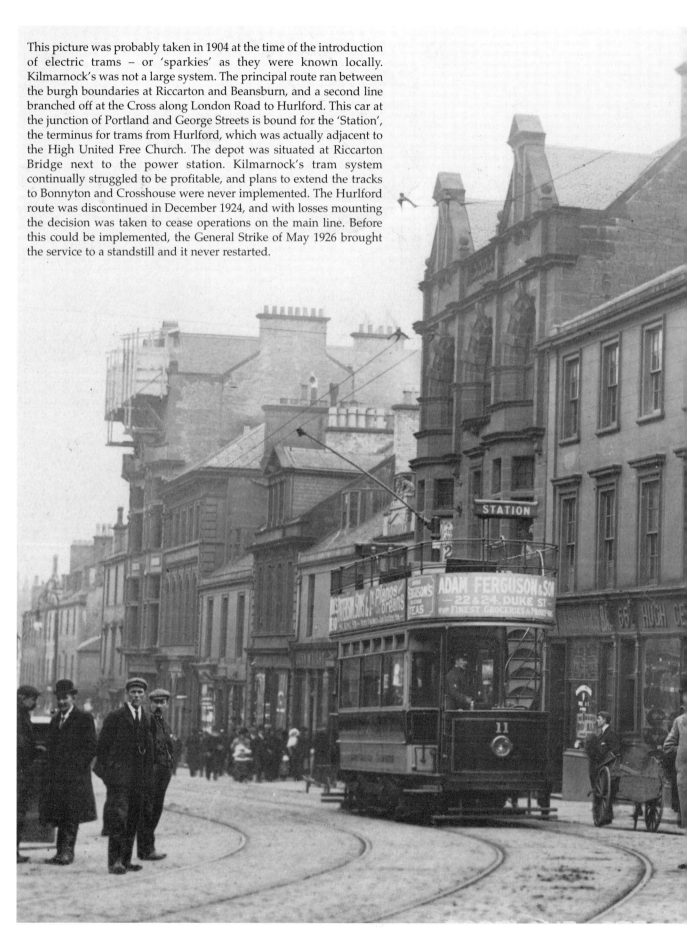

Following the demise of the trams, Kilmarnock Corporation started a bus service on the Hurlford route using four Albion vehicles. One of these is seen here in Wishaw prior to delivery in December 1924. Within a few weeks another eight buses had joined the fleet. They were painted in a similar livery to the trams, with olive green on the lower body, cream above, and a deep yellow band in between carrying the Kilmarnock Corporation name.

Private bus operators also established themselves in the town, and the Scottish General Transport Company opened a bus station on the corner of Portland and East George Streets in October 1923. The site had become vacant in 1921 when the previous occupant, the drapery warehouse of A. Ross & Co., was destroyed by fire.

The new station had garaging for about twenty buses, body and repair shops, offices, a waiting room and platforms. Buses entered from East George Street and left by way of Portland Street, which is visible beyond this line-up of vehicles.

This view of Portland Street, taken about 1930, shows the bus station on the left with John Craig & Sons' furnishing, upholstery and cabinetmaker's store next to it. This had been erected in 1904 to replace a smaller building. The bus industry also continued to evolve, and during a period of acquisitions and takeovers in the early thirties the Scottish General Transport Company became part of the Scottish Motor Traction Company (SMT). On 1 January 1932 SMT also took over Kilmarnock Corporation's bus services, and later that year Western SMT was formed as the local operating company. The Portland Street station became its headquarters. Following nationalisation in 1949, SMT became part of the Scottish Bus Group, although it retained the Western SMT name. The bus station was closed in 1979 and a replacement built off Green Street.

Dairy engineers and utensil-makers Walker & Templeton were based in Portland Street, although these tinsmiths were probably photographed at the company's workshops in Fore Street. Walker & Templeton also did sheet metalwork for other industries and operated as plumbers and heating engineers. This willingness to tackle a variety of tasks served the business well over the years, and it adapted to changing times by totally altering its product range. One of the town's great survivors, it entered the twenty-first century selling, among other things, school uniforms – a far cry from troughs and milk churns! Some of the company's early dairy equipment can be seen on page 43.

The Cross looks remarkably quiet in this early 1950s view looking towards Portland Street. By this time the distinctive Royal Bank of Scotland building had appeared on the corner of Fore Street. Built to the designs of W.K. Walker Todd in 1937–9, the interior had a marble mosaic floor depicting a threepenny bit, a twelve sided, nickel-brass coin introduced in 1937. This superseded a tiny silver coin of the same value, and although the old threepenny bits ceased to be minted after 1941 large numbers remained in circulation. They were often wrapped in greaseproof paper and put into birthday cakes for excited children to find.

The Royal Bank of Scotland replaced the attractive bow-fronted building on the left of this view. The narrow and less-than-straight road to its right was Fore Street, formerly Foregate, where one of Robert Burns' closest friends, Robert Muir, occupied a wing of the gushet house – the Portland Arms pub in this picture.

The street on the other side of the pub, Regent Street, led to Clerk's Lane where a church was erected in 1777 for a secession congregation. The original secession from the Established Church of Scotland took place in 1733 and the resulting church subsequently split into a number of factions. James Morison, minister at Clerk's Lane, precipitated another division in 1841 when he published a tract that so upset church leaders they suspended him on charges of 'heresy and disingenuous conduct'. That led to the formation of a new church known as the Evangelical Union, which used the Clerk's Lane building until the healing of church divisions created surplus accommodation. When it ceased to be required for worship it stood empty for a while and was then used as a cinema called the Electric Picture House for about two decades. It was demolished in 1938 to make way for a car park.

Duke Street was one of the 'new' streets that was opened up in Kilmarnock at the end of the 1850s. It is fondly remembered as one of turrets and towers, an image that is evident in this picture from around 1900. The display of assorted utensils, tin trunks and birdcages around the door of Christie's ironmongery store conveys an image of domestic life from another age. In the lower picture, taken after the tram services had been discontinued, Christie's has also moved on and instead of cages for singing birds is offering such advances in entertainment as the 'wireless'. The corner block, on the right, has been rebuilt and the ground floor occupied as a shop. This later became a branch of the North of Scotland Bank.

The North of Scotland and Clydesdale Banks were affiliated in 1950, and in 1963, the year after this picture was taken, the 'North' was dropped. To the bank's left are the offices of the *Kilmarnock Standard*, while further left again is Hay's, a furniture retailer from Ayr. This took over the local business of Messrs Richardson in 1936. Providing a focal point at the end of the street is the Corn Exchange and Palace Theatre building, with its imposing Albert Tower. It all made for a splendid urban setting, but just over a decade after this picture was taken Duke Street was demolished to make way for the new bus station, Burns shopping mall and ring-road. The Corn Exchange remained, but half hidden and somewhat isolated from the town centre, it no longer provided a keynote view. Duke Street is seen below about 1912 looking back towards the Cross from Green Street, with the Corn Exchange casting a shadow on the cobbles and tram tracks in the foreground.

The Cross in 1950 with Duke Street beyond.

As this picture of the Cross in the 1920s shows, one of its amenities was a subterranean gentlemen's toilet, something that was once found on many town and city street corners. These facilities were often dark, damp and smelly, but better than nothing, which was usually what was provided for women. The toilet railings cradle the statue of Sir James – or 'Jimmie' – Shaw. Born in 1764, he was a farmer's son from Riccarton who became the archetypal local boy made good. He spent time in America before pursuing a successful business career in London, becoming Lord Mayor of the city, an MP and a baronet. The statue was erected in 1848, but removed to another site in 1929 to improve traffic control. When the Cross was pedestrianised, Sir Jimmie was not reinstated, and his former place was taken by a statue of Robert Burns and other cronies. This honouring of the national bard, instead of the successful entrepreneur (who incidentally provided funds for Burns' widow, Jean Armour, after the poet's death) is an interesting reflection of our changing national tastes. Graffiti added to the plinth might indicate the shifting values of a new generation!

Waterloo Street, seen here about 1905 looking towards the town green, had strong connections with Robert Burns. John Wilson, who published that first and only 'Kilmarnock' edition of Burns' poems in 1786, had a shop in a part of the street that was obliterated a few years later to make way for the new King Street. The rest of Waterloo Street, including the Star Inn Close, where Wilson had his printing works, was demolished in the 1970s to make way for the Burns shopping mall. So despite having significant heritage value, Waterloo Street is no more.

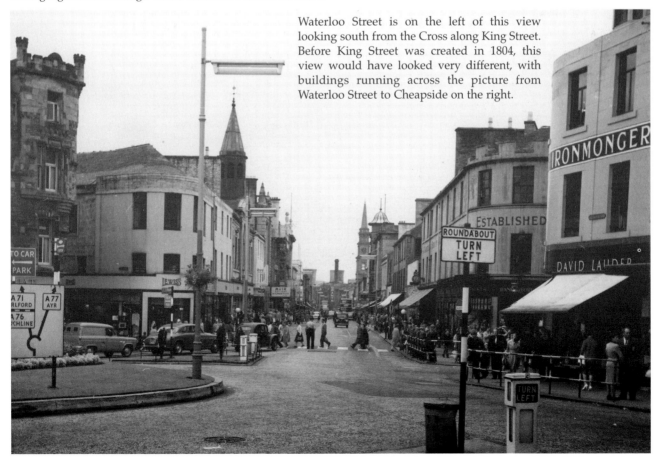

Waterloo Street is on the left of this view looking south from the Cross along King Street. Before King Street was created in 1804, this view would have looked very different, with buildings running across the picture from Waterloo Street to Cheapside on the right.

Sandbed formed part of the main north-south route through the town before King Street was opened up. It is seen here about 1900 from the Timmer Bridge, thought to be so-named because it was originally built of timber. Today the view has lost its picturesque quality with large shop buildings stretching between King Street and Sandbed, partly obscuring the Laigh Kirk. The church's tower is no longer reflected in still water as the weir in the foreground, built in the 1820s, was removed in the 1960s.

The unlovely backs of commercial buildings have given modern Sandbed the appearance of a drab service lane, but these pictures show that it was once a residential street with houses in the characterful Scots vernacular style. Latterly these buildings look to have been in a poor state, and this tenement appears to have had few amenities and many occupants when the photograph was taken.

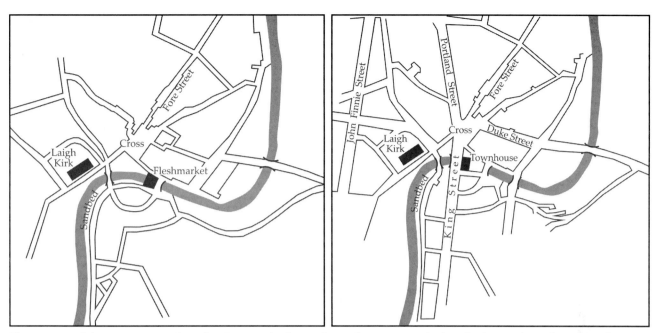

These maps of the area surrounding the Cross in the late eighteenth century and a hundred years later show how the town centre altered during that time. With new streets radiating from it in all directions, the Cross became more of a hub than it had been before. The biggest physical change was the covering of the river to create King Street. Prior to that the Kilmarnock Water was spanned by the Town's Bridge, which linked Sandbed and Cheapside, and by the Fleshmarket Bridge to the east. The latter was so-named because the market was built beside it over the water. In the days before proper drainage systems, this arrangement would have made it easier to dispose of effluent, which would simply have been slopped through the floor into the river. In later years the small section of river between the Fleshmarket and Green Street Bridges was also covered.

The way in which the river was covered allowed both sides of King Street to be developed as if the water wasn't there. The Town House, the building with the pointed spire whose entrance is flanked by shops, was built directly above the river. Designed by Robert Johnstone, it was noted for some fine stained glass windows.

The Town House, which is also prominent in this view looking south along King Street, was demolished as part of the town centre redevelopment of the 1970s. With such extensive rebuilding being carried out at the time, it seems a pity that the opportunity wasn't taken to open up the river again as a potentially attractive town centre feature. Instead, its position below King Street's pedestrian precinct is marked by sculptures of a fish and divers' heads, although the aquatic symbolism is probably lost on uninformed visitors. The picture dates from about 1920 and shows the bustle and activity of that time, with a couple of trams in the distance.

This picture was taken before the trams added to the clutter of people and carts in King Street, and the shops reflect the fashions of the time. Behind the awning in the centre of the picture the Misses Adams traded as ladies' outfitters. Next door (nearer the camera) was the Home & Colonial Tea Company, with Jackson and Co.'s fancy warehouse alongside. Gartshore & Douglas, at the extreme right-hand edge of the picture, was one of the town's major early retailers, founded as the Kilmarnock Drapery Warehouse by John M. Gartshore. His first shop was in Bank Street, but when trade outgrew those premises he moved to King Street.

Commercial House, to the right of centre, was the premises of the Commercial Bank. The building was remodelled in 1893, at which time the bank shared the ground floor frontage with a tenant, George Y. Bain & Sons. The Bains were drapers, clothiers and general outfitters who perpetuated a business begun in 1852 by a John Cadzow. They also used the upper floors and carried out tailoring in premises behind the bank. Next to Commercial House was a fruit merchant, McLauchlan & Co., and beside them, at the right-hand edge of the picture, was tobacconist and snuff merchant William Mitchell.

George Y. Bain & Sons ceased trading in 1938 when the Commercial Bank decided to reconstruct its building again. The imposing new edifice, just to the right of centre, is seen here in 1950. Major retailers like Boots (right) had moved into the street by then, alongside Scottish concerns such as the Maypole Dairy and Birrell's. Next to Birrell's, on the left, was the millinery and drapery shop of William K. Gailey & Co. which was destroyed by fire in 1954. The heat was so intense it smashed the plate glass windows of other shops and blistered several pianos in Paterson's music shop, on the extreme left on the near side of Water Lane.

The low-rise frontage of the Claude Alexander shop in this 1936 picture of King Street (looking south) indicates the location of the river below. Further along on the right-hand side, with a prominent sale notice outside, is Lauder's Emporium. This was opened in 1864 as a drapery store by Hugh Lauder. From those small beginnings it grew to become a local institution, even surviving a major fire in February 1923, after which it traded temporarily in the Agricultural Hall while the King Street store was rebuilt.

Lauder's restaurant and bakery shop is on the left of this almost identical view from 1951. The bakery started out as a family concern, but was transformed into a larger business when David Lauder took over its management in 1869. The spire of King Street Church is a distinctive feature in the distance, as is the Arts and Crafts style turret of the Victoria Buildings, erected on the corner of Sandbed Lane in 1901 to the designs of architect Thomas Smellie.

King Street was still a thriving shopping street when these pictures (looking north) were taken in the early 1960s. Hugh Lauder's Emporium is on the left of this view, opposite Woolworth's, which is still present on King Street but in a shop closer to the Cross. The buildings on the east (right) side of the street have all been replaced by the Burns shopping mall and subsequent developments.

The west side of King Street fared better in the planning lottery of the 1970s, with most of the buildings seen here on the left surviving. The more modern looking three-storey structure in the centre of the picture, at the corner of Water Lane, was built on the site of William K. Gailey's shop, which was destroyed by fire in 1954 (see page 21).

Despite the crowds, the tram in this picture of King Street looks empty, which suggests that the picture was taken just before the start of the service in 1904. People seem unconcerned about straying on to the road, a practice that would have been foolhardy later in the century, but which became normal again when this section of street was pedestrianised. Behind the crowd on the left, on the corner of St Marnock Street, is Norman Adam's baker's shop and restaurant – a customer is seated at a table in the first floor window. William Murdoch, next door, was a bookseller. Then came grocer David Boyd, confectioner John Stephen and tobacconist Alex Stevenson. Next to his shop was a painter, an upholsterer, the dyers Gibson & Reid and Jamieson the jeweller. Grocer Thomas Neil was on the corner with Bridge Lane. It was a typically varied block of King Street shops.

On the other side of the street, and a little further down, was Tommy Rodger's Picture Postcard Emporium, where many illustrations featured in this book would have been bought as postcards. The shop must have been a treasure trove, with local views on sale alongside Mr Rodger's more idiosyncratic creations, like the political cartoon on page 58. Customers also could get any newspaper they wanted or choose a sixpenny novel from over 10,000 titles. In addition the shop sold albums, purses, scraps, violin strings, games and photo frames.

King Street shops may have been smaller the further they were from the Cross, but they still offered a remarkable range of goods, including ironmongery, hats, meat, wine and children's clothing. In the left foreground of this 1920s view is the drysaltery of John Boyle Ltd., a shop set up in the 1870s. Next door is George Paterson's grocery – formerly John Ferguson's – also an old-established business. The large building with the bowed corner windows beyond is King Street Church.

King Street Church is also on the right of this picture of a bus working the old tramway route between Riccarton and Beansburn.

King Street Church came into existence after a dispute at Riccarton Parish Church in 1799. The congregation believed that the patron, Sir William Cunninghame of Caprington, was willing to let them select their own minister when a vacancy arose. They duly did so, only to discover he had chosen someone already. The Established Church of Scotland upheld the patron's right, but many parishioners refused to accept this and left. They became a congregation of the Relief Church, which had broken away from the Establishment in 1762 to provide relief to parishioners in dispute with their patron. The Kilmarnock congregation's first church was at Riccarton, but they moved from there to a new church in King Street in 1814, and then replaced this about 1832 with the building in the picture. It was demolished in 1966.

The Empire Cinema, on the right of this view of Titchfield Street, opened in 1913 as the first purpose-built cinema in the town. It had 600 seats, including couches on the balcony. The Empire was popular with the town's moviegoers, but as an independent cinema it struggled to get new films and was looking somewhat tired when it closed in 1964. The building remained in use for another two years as a bingo hall before burning down.

The Empire was built alongside the 2,000 seat King's Theatre, which had opened in 1904. Its splendid red sandstone frontage reflected confidence, but the owners were soon in financial difficulties and had to sell. After that the theatre continued to struggle as a live performance venue, gradually giving way to movies. In the 1930s it was modernised and reopened as the Regal Picture House. It was unable to survive the impact of television in the 1970s and closed to become a bingo hall. A fire brought a swift end to that venture, but after a makeover the building reopened as a three-screen cinema, remaining in business for a little over twenty years before it too closed.

MOLLIE LINDSAY

MOLLIE LINDSAY

Mollie Lindsay, whose real surname was McVie and whose father was bandmaster at the Industrial School, grew up in Kilmarnock and went to the High Street and Kay Schools. As a young woman she moved to London where she worked in business for six or seven years. In 1912 she was offered the part of Effie Robertson in a new Scottish domestic sketch, *The Washing House Key*. She hadn't considered a stage career before, but the sketch's debut London run was so successful that she bought the rights, formed a company and started to tour the halls. She appeared at the Palace Theatre in Kilmarnock in 1913, returning with her company to the King's in April 1915. Styled as 'Kilmarnock's Ain Lassie', and coming 'direct from the principal London halls', Mollie was accompanied by Harriet Callander, a 'Well Known Vocalist', Donald MacKay, 'Scotland's Premier Patter Comedian', Maggie McIntosh, 'the Dainty Comedienne', and the Great Rauli, a 'Marvel of Mystery and Wonderful Contortionist'.

Titchfield Street was named after the Marquis of Titchfield, who became the 4th Duke of Portland in 1809. It is seen here in the 1930s looking north, with Armour Street on the right. Young's Stores, on the corner, was a hardware shop which later moved to John Finnie Street. Two important civic structures, the fire station and swimming baths, were built further up the street on the right-hand side and replaced some of the smaller buildings. Butcher R. Ferguson sold his famous Glencairn Pies for a mere sixpence from one of these.

The success of industrial shoemaking in Kilmarnock was based on the simple concept of manufacturing footwear that actually fitted the width and length of people's feet. It was developed by Clark & Co., which had been making shoes since 1820. Clark's was the forerunner of the Saxone Shoe Company, which was formed early in twentieth century and quickly became known around the world for its fine footwear. The company opened a second works in Mill Street in 1949 to make shoes for women and children, while the original factory, seen here from Howard Park in 1921, concentrated on making men's shoes. After its closure the Galleon Centre leisure complex was built on the site. On the right of the picture is Douglas Street, leading to Titchfield Street.

The main north-south road which bisects the peninsula formed by the Kilmarnock Water and the River Irvine was laid out as straight as an arrow in 1765. It runs for about 1,000 yards and has four names: Titchfield Street, High Glencairn Street, Glencairn Square and Low Glencairn Street. High Glencairn Street is seen here looking south in 1921. This area was formerly known as Netherton – the nether, or lower town. A fire here in 1800, caused by an overheated kiln, destroyed so much property that the opportunity was taken to clear the debris and lay the area out anew.

Glencairn Square, seen here looking north in 1921, was formerly known as Holm Square. It was an attractive urban space, much of which was later demolished. The north-east corner, shown here, is now occupied by a Lidl supermarket.

Sluice Gates for Hydro-Electric control

THE illustration is an upstream view of the Glenlochar Sluice Gate Barrage situated at the foot of Loch Ken, and used to regulate the storage of water for use on the extensive Hydro-Electric scheme now nearing completion in the Galloway district.

The six Glenfield Free Roller Sluice Gates installed on this Barrage are each 45′ 0′ span by 10′ 0′ deep, and were made and erected by us for The Galloway Water Power Company.

Other recent contracts carried out by us include sluice gates and valves for the Laggan Dam of the Lochaber Hydro-Electric Scheme extensions, sluice gates for the Rannoch and Tummel Barrages of the Grampian Hydro-Electric Scheme extensions and 11′ 6″ diameter valves for the Tongueland Power Station of the Galloway Scheme.

Glenfield Hydro-Electric Control Equipment is installed on all the major Hydro-Electric Schemes hitherto developed in this country, and also on many schemes in the Dominions and abroad.

Write for descriptive pamphlet of Hydro-Electric Equipment sent free on request.

GLENFIELD AND KENNEDY LIMITED KILMARNOCK

The area between Low Glencairn Street and the River Irvine was dominated by one company, Glenfield & Kennedy. This owed its origins to Thomas Kennedy, who formed the Kennedy Water Meter Company in 1852 after patenting a design for a meter. Another business, the Glenfield Company, was set up in 1865 to make castings for the meters, but over time broadened its manufacturing base. The two came together in 1899 as Glenfield & Kennedy, expanding to become the largest engineering company in the British Commonwealth. Products included valves and other water control equipment, and the company also undertook large-scale projects such as the construction of barrages and other elements of hydro-electric schemes (as shown in the advertisement from 1933 on the facing page). The works eventually grew to cover 26 acres.

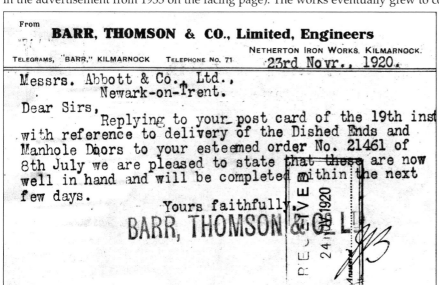

From **BARR, THOMSON & CO., Limited, Engineers**

NETHERTON IRON WORKS, KILMARNOCK.

TELEGRAMS, "BARR," KILMARNOCK   TELEPHONE NO. 71   23rd Novr., 1920.

Messrs. Abbott & Co., Ltd.,
            Newark-on-Trent.

Dear Sirs,
            Replying to your post card of the 19th inst with reference to delivery of the Dished Ends and Manhole Doors to your esteemed order No. 21461 of 8th July we are pleased to state that these are now well in hand and will be completed within the next few days.

                    Yours faithfully,

BARR, THOMSON & CO L

James Barr's engineering business was established in 1884 and became Barr, Thomson & Co. in 1900. It made a range of iron and steel products at the Netherton Iron Works on Kirkstyle Road, situated roughly on the site of the Asda car park at Queen's Drive retail park.

Like the Kilmarnock Water, the River Irvine was spanned by numerous weirs which were built to harness water power to drive mills. This weir was to the east of Riccarton, located roughly where the northern ramps of the large interchange on the A77 are today. Although indistinct, Riccarton Mill can be seen in the centre of the picture. It was fed by a lade from a weir above the railway viaduct, which can also be made out in the background.

Water from the weir in the upper picture was fed along a lade which cleverly cut off a bend in the river. This lade powered a corn mill, known as New Mill because it superseded the town's old mill. New Mill Road perpetuates the name, and the site remains in use as business premises.

Much of Kilmarnock's early industry was based on textile-making, but in 1728 a Miss Maria Gardiner gave another activity a boost when she brought carpet spinners and weavers from Dalkeith to the town to impart their skills. Carpets were still made on hand looms at the time, so the industry initially remained small-scale. It gradually developed, until by the 1820s Kilmarnock was employing twice as many carpet weavers as the rest of the country put together. One man who pioneered improvements was Thomas Morton. He devised what became known as three-ply Scotch carpets, which had a finished appearance on both sides. People often used them with the dark side showing during the winter months and the light side in summer. The last major manufacturer in the town was BMK – Blackwood & Morton, Kilmarnock – formed in 1908. The building of its impressive Burnside Works in the 1930s allowed the company to quadruple its workforce and massively increase output.

Exact identification of this picture is tricky. It was sent to Glasgow in 1909 and has a Kilmarnock postmark, suggesting that it shows a Blackwood & Morton loom. The sender describes it as 'our largest and best machine, 360 inches wide' (360 inches = 9.15 metres). The works continued to thrive until about 1980, when cheap imports began to have a negative impact on sales. As losses mounted the future looked uncertain. The prospect of a management buyout offered hope for a while, but in 1992 the Stoddart Sekers Group moved in to take over the company, retaining some carpet-making in the town.

Kilmarnock's coal-fired power station began generating electricity for the tram system and other users in 1904. It was built adjacent to Riccarton Bridge on the site of an old mill. The riverside location had already been developed for the use of water, which was essential to the power station for cooling. Ten years after the station opened, Kilmarnock Corporation was given permission to extend its area of supply to a large part of north Ayrshire. When Ayr's power station closed in 1924, Kilmarnock became the generating station for the whole county. Having been upgraded and extended regularly, it was connected to the national grid in 1932 and became part of the nationalised supply industry under the Electricity (Supply) Act of 1947. It was decommissioned in the 1970s.

Stepping stones and a ford were used to cross the River Irvine before Riccarton Bridge was built in 1723. This in turn was superseded by a new bridge, erected in 1835–8, seen here with the village of Riccarton behind.

Riccarton was a typical old Scots village, set beside a river and located between a kirk and a castle. Nothing of the latter survives, although a plaque claims that the fire station was built on its site. The castle is thought to have been the seat of Richard Wallace, who was granted the lands in the twelfth century. The village took his name, Richardstown, later corrupted to Riccarton. Richard was a forebear or close relative of the Scottish patriot William Wallace, whose father, Malcolm, is thought to have been born at Riccarton. Some also claim it as the birthplace of the hero himself. When Riccarton became part of Kilmarnock in 1832, Old Street was the centre of the village, with shops, pubs, and as these pictures clearly show, the kirk sitting on top of its hill.

Riccarton Kirk, with its distinctive spire and unusual pediment, was built to the designs of architect John Richmond in 1823 to replace an older structure. Grants from Historic Scotland and the Heritage Lottery Fund have helped with its upkeep. Once the parish church for a sparsely populated rural area, its congregation was later swollen by the influx of miners, drawn to the village by the opening up of nearby coal reserves.

Campbell Street, created in the 1830s to align with the new bridge, is seen here during the tramway era with a passing loop evident in the track layout. Transport services were just one of Riccarton's links with its larger neighbour. The village's population grew during Kilmarnock's years of industrial expansion, and in the 1940s and 50s new council housing schemes encircled the old village. Neglect and decay caused concern in the 1970s, but the ultimate insult came in the 1980s when the A71 dual carriageway to Irvine was driven across Old and Campbell Streets on a flyover. There was mud everywhere, while blocked footpaths and damaged street lighting caused further misery for villagers.

The street furniture and distant cottages have been replaced, but otherwise little has changed since this picture of Craigie Road was taken in the 1920s. As such this is one of the few bits of old Riccarton to have been relatively unscathed by the predations of the late twentieth century planners.

This lodge or gatehouse guarded the entrance to Treesbank, an estate to the south of Riccarton. Sir Hugh Campbell of Cessnock gave Treesbank to his son, James, on the occasion of his marriage to Jean Mure of Rowallan in 1672. George James Campbell, who inherited the estate in 1815, altered and enlarged the house in 1838 to give it the appearance seen here. Although the Campbells were one of the principal families in the county, their hold on the estate eventually ended and it was acquired by Gavin Morton of BMK carpets. In 1926 he rebuilt the house in Tudor style. It was bought by the Glasgow Trades Council in 1975, and used by the Scottish Trades Union Congress as a conference centre until 1991.

Kilmarnock's first municipal golf course was opened to the south of Riccarton in 1909. It was laid out for the town council by a David Kilpatrick, who later set up a golf shop, seen in the centre of this picture. Two golfers are teeing off, to the evident excitement of the dogs on the left. Would such behaviour be tolerated on what is now known as Caprington Golf Course?

To the north-west of the golf course is Caprington Castle, a mansion built in 1829 (although an earlier castle is thought to have stood on or near the site). The Caprington name has become more widely known thanks to a beam engine from the nearby mine which has been re-erected as an exhibit in the Museum of Scotland in Edinburgh.

Bellfield House, a Georgian mansion to the east of Riccarton, was bought in the early to mid nineteenth century by three sisters, Margaret, Jane and Elizabeth Buchanan. Their father had been a successful businessman in Glasgow with connections to James Finlay & Co., an enterprise in which one of their brothers, James, was a partner. He was unmarried and so the sisters inherited both his and their father's wealth. It is not known why three rich and apparently comely women remained single, but they instructed their lawyer in Glasgow to draw up a will which left the estate and house, complete with furnishings, family portraits and about 1,500 books, to 'the people of Kilmarnock and Riccarton as a place of recreation in all time coming'. The last of the ladies could have made alterations, but Elizabeth, who died in 1875, remained true to her sisters' wishes. Ten years later the full terms of the will were implemented, and the Bellfield Trust, officially known as the 'Royal Incorporation of the Buchanan Bequest', was set up to administer it.

With the construction of the Reid Bridge in 1883, and its replacement by the Victoria Bridge and Queen's Drive, the estate became easily accessible from the town centre and people became fond of saying 'let's walk out to Bellfield'. It was a popular place for private picnics, as well as organised events such as the religious rally seen in the lower picture. Described by a late nineteenth century commentator as a 'a possession of which any town might be proud', it remained in good order for about sixty years. However, by the 1950s the estate had been earmarked for the construction of 1,850 council houses, and serious concerns were being expressed about the future of the mansion house. People were right to be worried: ravaged by the twin evils of neglect and vandalism, this precious gift was demolished in 1970.

These days, people often think about milk only in terms of the difference of a few pence in supermarket prices, but the issues were more serious in 1889 when a combination of dairy associations in the south and west of Scotland founded the Scottish Dairy Institute. There was a desire to improve hygiene, promote good practice and modernise the industry in the face of growing competition from abroad. With financial assistance from landowners who had an interest in dairy production, the institute raised funds to fit up and maintain part of the steading at Holmes Farm as a dairy school. Ayrshire was the natural home for such a school; it was Scotland's principal milk-producing area, and its farmers had developed the Ayrshire breed of dairy cattle, famed for its high milk yield. The pictures on these pages show the school after its expansion in 1904.

When first opened in 1889 the school had three rooms for making, pressing and curing cheeses, and two rooms for butter-making. One of these had stone benches to provide cool conditions for settling and raising the cream, while the other was used to churn and finish the butter. Ten years later, the school was incorporated into the Glasgow-based West of Scotland Agricultural College. The college established an experiment station at the farm where different varieties of cereal crops, potatoes and grasses were tried out, along with ways of cultivating them. Meanwhile, the dairy school remained the only establishment of its kind in the country and its size restricted the number of students that could be taught at any one time. As a result, plans were drawn up for a larger institution, and this was opened as the Dairy School for Scotland by Lord Howard de Walden in June 1904.

The new dairy school was designed by the architect Allan Stevenson of Ayr. It could accommodate 80 students and had spacious rooms for making butter, cheese and soft cheese, as well as a press room, balance room and cellarage for coating purposes. There was a lecture hall, chemical laboratories and space for botanical and bacteriological work, plus a new poultry farm. Despite this physical expansion, concerns remained about the West of Scotland Agricultural College's organisational structure. It was still split between its original site in Glasgow and Holmes Farm, and by the start of the 1920s this arrangement was becoming restrictive. The search for a new, unified location ended in 1927 when the offer to relocate to Auchencruive Estate was accepted. The Duke of York formally opened the new college in July 1931, and a few years later the vacated Holmes Farm became the site of Kilmarnock's maternity home.

A different kind of activity dedicated to the needs of agriculture developed just after the Second World War. With the British economy in a parlous state, the Board of Trade sought to control the flow of money into the dollar area by asking Canadian harvesting machine manufacturers to set up in Britain. Massey-Harris responded by opening one factory in Manchester in 1945 and selecting the site for another at Moorfield, to the west of Kilmarnock. Company president, James S. Duncan, a man of Scottish descent, was happy to establish a presence in his old homeland. Tractor assembly began in October 1949, as soon as the roof was on the first section of the works. The formal opening ceremony took place in November, followed by a celebratory lunch, which was almost marred by someone who threw an untidy-looking half-opened parcel into a furnace in the rush to make the works look as clean as possible. It contained the menu cards, emblazoned with a replica of the bronze company seal, but a local printer saved the day by producing something similar at very short notice.

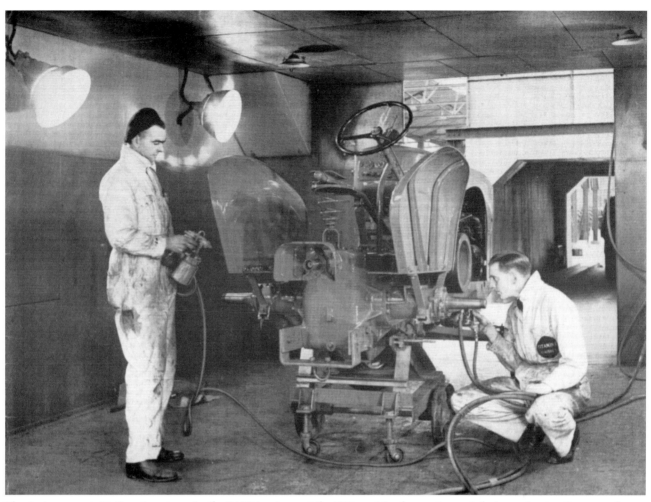

The factory was initially set up to make the 744D tractor and the 726 combine harvester, and their production lines are shown on these pages. Painters are seen spraying a tractor body at the top of this page, while the picture at the foot shows the exterior of the works. The factory's opening was universally welcomed, but three years later the farm machinery world was shocked by the news that Massey-Harris was to amalgamate with rival Harry Ferguson. He was known as an ideas man, but one who was difficult to work with. Despite this, one Ayrshire farmer was impressed. Driving his Ferguson tractor along a road, he was stopped by Harry Ferguson, who when told about a problem with the brakes took the tractor for a drive, diagnosed the difficulty, and not only sorted that machine but incorporated a modification in manufacture. The new company became known as Massey-Ferguson and the Kilmarnock works, which was well placed to meet domestic and export orders, continued to thrive.

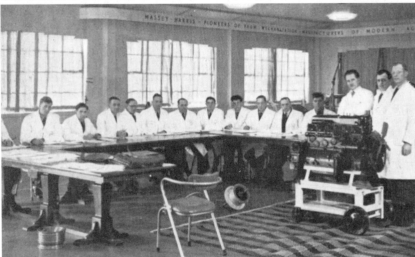

Massey-Ferguson was a modern concern, but one night a blacksmith employed by the company caused consternation when he was found shoeing a horse in the middle of the works. He had asked permission, but the foreman, always in a rush, hadn't stopped to listen and had some explaining to do. As well as making farm machinery (and shoeing the odd horse) the factory incorporated a School of Service Instruction, where dealers and service-men spent a week learning about the company's products and their maintenance. Lessons started on the Monday morning at 9 a.m. sharp and finished at 5.30 on the Friday afternoon. Anyone coming from a distance had to arrive by the Sunday evening and leave on the Saturday. At its height, Massey-Ferguson employed up to 2,000 people and paid good wages compared with other industries. This could have had a destabilising effect on employment in the town, but in the end Massey-Ferguson's own workforce became disaffected as the euphoria of the early days began to unravel. Industrial disputes grew, and the company eventually decided to cut its losses and move elsewhere. The lower picture shows the demolition of the works in 1984.

The tractor factory was sited close to the railway line between Kilmarnock and Troon, and tracks led into the works so that machinery bound for export could be moved by rail to the Glasgow docks, although in practice the facility was rarely used. The company had a scrapyard adjacent to Gatehead Station, and this came in handy for a local farmer and skilled engineer who built a baler from parts liberated from the yard, something like the man in the Johnnie Cash song who assembled a Cadillac 'one piece at a time'. This picture shows Gatehead Station on a particularly wet day.

A substantial wall, built as a flood defence measure, means it would be impossible to replicate this photograph of Fairyhill Road today. Prior to the wall's construction the houses were prone to flooding by the Kilmarnock Water. The road was on the edge of Holmes Farm where the Fairy Hill was a well-known feature.

McLelland Drive is seen here at its southern end before the First World War, with Fairyhill Road to the left and the entrance to Howard Park on the right. Named after Archibald McLelland, who was provost from 1886 to 1895, the drive was developed in the early 1900s as one of a series of streets forming an early town centre bypass between Glencairn Square and Bonnyton. The bridge to West Shaw Street, in the foreground, was built in 1888 by one of Kilmarnock's foremost engineering companies, Grant, Ritchie & Co. (see page 69). It was rebuilt and more than doubled in width in the 1920s, formally reopening in February 1923. McLelland Drive is seen below in November 1924 with Scott Road on the left. The view has been significantly altered by the enlargement of Rugby Park, which now dominates the skyline behind the houses in the background.

Football wasn't always Scotland's national game. In the mid-nineteenth century sport was a summer activity, with cricket both popular and widespread, but the enforced idleness of autumn and winter prompted sportsmen to look around for another game. Kilmarnock Football Club, formed in 1869, was typical of this trend. Initially its members played rugby on a field which people quickly started to call Rugby Park. However, the team soon switched to Association Football, which was evolving rapidly, and transferred to a more suitable pitch at Grange. There, according to an early account of the club, 'as a band of noble warriors they were second to none, but as footballers they were second to almost anything'. In 1876 the club began sharing a ground with the cricketers at Holm Quarry, but a dispute over rent saw them return first to Grange and then to Rugby Park. In 1884 the club won both the Ayrshire Cup and the Kilmarnock Charity Cup, and began to make this something of a habit. Its stature grew in season 1896/97 when it beat Motherwell for the Scottish Qualifying Cup, and also competed in the Second Scottish League for the first time, coming third. Kilmarnock won the competition the following two seasons, gaining promotion to the First League. Since those early days the club has been one of the country's more successful outfits outside the big cities, with victories in the Scottish Cup in 1920 and 1929. Kilmarnock also memorably won the Scottish League in 1964/65.

Left: Robert Beattie was a Kilmarnock lad who played at inside forward for the club between 1932 and 1937.

Right: Kilmarnock born Douglas Haig McAvoy played at inside left for the club between 1936 and 1948.

The team picture for season 1906/07 shows:
 Back row: G. Fullarton, W. Shaw, F. Frew (secretary), D. MacCallum, W. Agnew
 Front row: T. Drain (kneeling), J. Maxwell, D. Howie, H. Monteith, S. Graham, H. Black (kneeling), W. Linward

The team picture for season 1922/23 shows:
 Back row: P. Carrick, M. Smith, D. Brown, W. Culley, A. Herron, J. Turnbull, W. Watson, J. Ramsay, J. McWhinnie
 Front row: J. Goldie, R. Howatt, W. Jackson, J. Hood, J. Harvey, D. Corbett, M. McLeavy, D. Gibson, M. McPhail

With Pointhouse on the left and a simple sign for Troon at the kerbside, Dundonald Road heads for the country in this picture from the mid-1930s.

Hamilton Street was developed during the last two decades of the nineteenth century. The portion now known as South Hamilton Street is seen here in the mid-1930s looking north from its junction with Dundonald Road. It was laid out across ground that had been part of Rugby Park before the football pitch was realigned and contained within terraces and stands.

The 125-acre Annanhill Estate was situated due west of the town centre. It became public parkland in 1930 with the gardens, surrounded by trees and walls of mellow red brick, providing a restful place to sit. For a few years in the early 1950s the mansion house, dating from 1796, was used as a social club for Massey-Harris employees and their families. When the grounds were laid out as an 18-hole golf course it became the clubhouse. It ceased to be used for that purpose in the late 1980s, and has since been turned into flats.

Dundonald Road is seen here looking towards John Finnie Street. Poking above the roofs of the houses on the right is the pinnacled tower of St Marnock's Church, while behind the tree and railings on the left are Winton Place Church and Holy Trinity Episcopal Church. The latter was erected in 1857 on the site of the terminus of one of Scotland's pioneering railways. Built by the 4th Duke of Portland to get coal to the coast, the Kilmarnock & Troon Railway was opened in 1812. Four years later it became the first railway in Scotland to try out a steam locomotive, but this broke the primitive plate-like rails and the trials were discontinued. With its place in history assured, Kilmarnock went on to become a major railway town.

Holy Trinity Episcopal Church is out of sight behind the wall and trees on the left of this 1936 view of Portland Road. On the right is Portland Road United Presbyterian Church, which was opened in December 1859 for a congregation whose first church had been established in Wellington Street in 1772. A new church, Howard St Andrews, was built on the site in 1970/71.

As the town's population grew, its existing places of worship couldn't cope with the increasing numbers of people and the Established Church of Scotland had to provide new churches. One of these was St Marnock's, erected in 1836 and the largest church building in the town. It was a chapel of ease, which meant that it was subordinate to the parish church. When large numbers of parishioners left during the Disruption of 1843, those remaining with the Established Church attended the parent church, resulting in the closure of St Marnock's. It reopened in 1859 and was elevated to parish church status three years later.

The Boyd family's principal residence, Dean Castle, was destroyed by fire in 1735, after which William Boyd, 4th Earl of Kilmarnock, moved his family into his townhouse, Kilmarnock House (above). Ten years later the earl was one of the few lowland lairds to join Bonnie Prince Charlie's Jacobite Rebellion, and when he was captured and executed the family lost their estates. James, the eldest son, who had fought on the government side, was able to reclaim the estate but not the earldom. On inheriting another title he sold his Kilmarnock lands to the Earl of Glencairn. He in turn sold them to General John Scott of Balgonie's daughter, Henrietta. In 1795 she married William Cavendish-Bentinck, Marquis of Titchfield, who became 4th Duke of Portland in 1809. The lands then passed through the female line to the Howard de Walden family. These aristocratic families saw the estate as a business and a responsibility which they managed benignly, leaving their mark both in terms of street names and progressive development. However, despite being a fine-looking building in the Scots vernacular style, none of the latter owners of Kilmarnock House appear to have had much interest in it. It was used as a boys' industrial school until the early 1920s, and was subsequently demolished. The former sheriff courthouse in St Marnock Street was built alongside Kilmarnock House in 1852 to the designs of architect William Railton. It was superseded by the new court in 1985 and subsequently restored for use as offices.

A small open space known as Barbadoes Green was expanded into a larger park when the Duke of Portland's sister, Baroness Howard de Walden, gifted additional land from the former grounds of Kilmarnock House to the town. The expanded area was named Howard Park. It is seen here in 1950 with the Old Men's Cabin on the left. The spire of King Street Church can be seen in the distance.

This view from 1936 shows the same path, but this time looking towards Wallace Street. The imposing memorial erected in 1896 to commemorate Dr Alexander Marshall's 42 years as a medical practitioner is out of sight to the right.

Howard Park's bandstand was like an outdoor stage, suited as much to the performances of travelling entertainers as to band music.

Before it became a place of recreation, the area taken in by Howard Park was silent witness to some melancholy events. In 1746, while her husband languished in a London jail awaiting trial and execution, Lady Boyd is said to have eased her anxiety by walking beside the river. The path became known as the Lady Walk. A century later, during the cholera epidemic that swept Scotland in 1832, so many people died in Kilmarnock that the churchyards couldn't cope and a corner of the future park became the site of a mass grave. A memorial stone marks the anonymous victims' burial place. The park is seen here from Dundonald Road with Wards Place, the Saxone factory and the sports pavilion in the background.

The Fifth Ward Terrier.

Politicians have always used the most up-to-date methods to publicise themselves, and in the early years of the twentieth century this meant the postcard. The fifth ward was the largely residential area south of Portland Road and west of the river: its 'terrier' was Baillie William Munro. He got into trouble in February 1904 when the town council received a letter, apparently from the Carnegie Foundation, offering a large sum of money for a Burns Temple. This turned out to be a hoax instigated by the baillie, who donated £50 to the infirmary in an attempt to quieten the controversy. When the fuss refused to die down he resigned. The voters, apparently unconcerned, returned him to the council at the next election in November.

When Arthur Balfour's Tory government resigned in December 1905, the Liberal Party, led by Glaswegian Sir Henry Campbell-Bannerman, accepted office and promptly called a general election. Dr A. Roland Rainy stood for the Liberals in Kilmarnock, and this campaign postcard was sent on 24 January 1906 – the day after the election – with a triumphant 'MP Kilmarnock Burghs' scrawled on the front and the message on the back reading: 'Had a splendid victory ... gained the seat with a 2,525 majority' – a thumping win in those days.

Dr. A. Roland Rainy. *M P Kilmarnock Burghs*

The Scottish Co-operative Wholesale Society (SCWS) existed principally to supply goods to retail co-operative societies. Its headquarters were at Shieldhall in Glasgow, but in 1878 it set up a depot in Kilmarnock. Local co-operators wanted a full-scale branch, as had been established at Leith, but the SCWS had concerns about the costs of moving imported goods to an inland town and only wanted a base to secure local produce. So it remained a depot, which moved to Grange and Woodstock Streets in 1882. The SCWS and Kilmarnock Equitable worked closely together in the supply of foodstuffs such as bread. This picture shows the flour store in Grange Street.

One the depot's main activities was the processing of pork, Ayrshire bacon being highly regarded. At the start of the Second World War nearly 1,000 pigs were being prepared a week, but the operation closed in 1942 following the Ministry of Food's decision to concentrate production at a few large factories. Some processing activity, like sausage-making (seen here) continued.

John Finnie's father, Archibald, had been provost of the town in the 1830s, and his brother, also Archibald, was provost from 1858–61. The family's wealth and influence came from the coal and iron industries, although John's money originated in other commercial ventures. He used some of it to pay for a new street which was laid out in 1864. Named John Finnie Street in his honour, it was to some extent an attempt to move the business heart of the town to the west, where it would be in close proximity to the station. It is seen here in the mid-1930s looking north from the junction with Dundonald and Portland Roads and St Marnock Street. Bank Street is on the right.

John Finnie Street (left) echoed the direction, if not the meandering line, of Bank Street, which is again on the right of this view from the 1970s. It shows the same junction as in the upper picture.

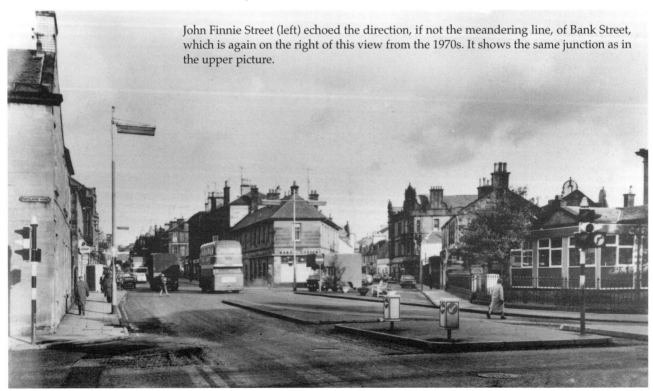

Most of the buildings in John Finnie Street were developed in the 1870s, including one known as the Opera House. This didn't quite enhance the town's cultural life as intended. It was used as a church and then business premises, before finally succumbing to fire in 1989. The Opera House somehow echoed the fate of the street as a whole, which never fully realised the lofty ambitions its promoters had for it. It did, however, acquire the appearance of a major commercial thoroughfare, as is evident from this picture looking towards the station from its junction with Grange and Bank Places.

Kilmarnock has been a centre for postal services since the 1660s, when it was on the mail route between Edinburgh and Ireland. Since then a number of premises have been used as the town's post office. This building, on the corner of John Finnie Street and Bank Place, took over from premises in Queen Street in 1878. The present post office, on the other side of the street, was opened in 1907. It was equipped with the most up-to-date means of communication: a public telephone booth, telegram writing tables and a telegraph instrument room. While these may have been superseded, the current KA postcode for Ayrshire reflects the town's continuing importance as a centre for postal services.

Bank Street takes its name from the Kilmarnock Bank Company, which opened its doors for business in 1802 but was taken over by the Ayr-based bank of Hunter's & Co. nineteen years later. It in turn became part of the Union Bank of Scotland in August 1843, an institution which had been set up in 1830 as the Glasgow Union Banking Company, but which changed its name a month before taking over Hunter's. This was to reflect its growing national status, achieved by absorbing a number of smaller Glasgow banks, as well as local banks in Paisley, Aberdeen, Perth and Ayrshire. The process of takeover and amalgamation continued in the 1950s, when the Union Bank became part of the Bank of Scotland. As a result of its branch closures there is now no bank in Bank Street, seen here looking north from the corner of Bank Place sometime around the 1970s.

The Strand, seen here with Dunlop Street on the left and Croft Street on the right, formed a small enclave tucked in behind John Finnie Street. The architecture, dominated as it was by Johnnie Walker's huge whisky bonds, was heroic in scale and quite unlike anything else in the town.

With red sandstone stipulated for all the buildings, John Finnie Street is regarded as an excellent example of a planned thoroughfare and – architecturally – as the town's finest street. This has been recognised by the award of a grant from the Heritage Lottery Fund's townscape heritage initiative to carry out restoration work in John Finnie and Bank Streets. One of the most distinctive buildings, on the corner with West George Street, was built in the 1880s and gifted to the town as a temperance hotel and restaurant by the 5th Duke of Portland's sister, Lady Ossington. Known as 'the Ossington', it seen in the left foreground of this mid-1930s picture, heroically marketing abstinence in the shadow of the Johnnie Walker bonded warehouses.

Early advertisements for Johnnie Walker had about as much punch as those for the Ossington.

Ossington Coffee Tavern,
JOHN FINNIE STREET,
KILMARNOCK.
(OPPOSITE RAILWAY STATION.)

BREAKFASTS, DINNERS, & TEAS,
Daily from 7 a.m to 10 p.m.

Ossington Reading Room.

> ⟶ ◆ ◆ ⟵

Annual Subscription, = = 10/6.
Country Members, = = = 5/=.

☞ STRANGERS, ONE PENNY PER VISIT.

I recommend

"JOHNNIE WALKER"

When John Walker was orphaned at the age of fourteen, his father's trustees sold the family farm, setting up a shop for him in King Street with the proceeds. This opened in 1820 and sold groceries, wines and spirits. John built up a successful business, but this was hit by the flood of July 1852 when a huge volume of water, held back by the town centre bridges, poured into the streets and swamped houses and shops. Much of his stock was lost, but by the time he died five years later John Walker's shop – still essentially a general grocery – had recovered. His son, Alexander, took control of the business and introduced a system whereby ships' captains were entrusted with a supply of whisky which they sold during a voyage, sharing the profit on their return. He also opened larger premises in Croft Street for blending and bottling whisky. Alexander died in 1889, but the expansion of the business carried on under his youngest son, also Alexander.

The pictures show the bottle washing house (upper) and the export bottling warehouse (lower), two activities which evidently employed women as well as men.

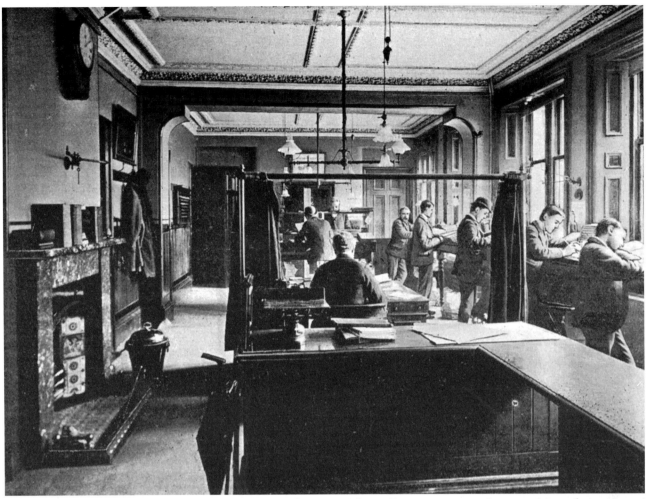

The scale of the Walker enterprise can be gauged from the number of men needed to keep the books in the counting house – counting was clearly men's work!

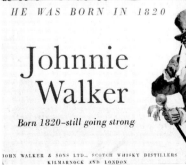

Throughout these early years the company produced one whisky, Walker's Old Highland Blend, but in 1906 Special Old Highland Whisky was introduced and given a red label. The original product was renamed Extra Special Old Highland Whisky. It had a black label, so unsurprisingly customers started asking for their whisky by the label colour. As a result the names Red Label and Black Label were adopted in 1909. A year earlier a commercial artist named Tom Browne had devised the striding man logo, and at the same time a company employee, James (later Lord) Stevenson, came up with the slogan 'Johnnie Walker: born 1820 – still going strong'. These innovations, coupled with the square bottles and angled labels, gave Johnnie Walker whisky a strong corporate identity well ahead of its time. In 1925 it became part of Distillers Company Limited (DCL) and in 1956 opened new premises in Hill Street. DCL was later taken over by Guinness and became part of the drinks conglomerate Diageo when this was formed in 1997.

The company's marketing image was transformed by the famous striding man figure, seen here celebrating the Coronation of 1953.

The main section of the Glasgow, Paisley, Kilmarnock & Ayr Railway ran between Ayr and Paisley and was opened in stages in 1839 and 1840. In 1843 it was connected to Kilmarnock by a line running from Dalry. Although initially a branch, this became a principal through route when the Glasgow, Dumfries & Carlisle Railway was completed in 1846. In less than ten years Kilmarnock had been connected by rail to Glasgow and all points south. With abundant coal, it was in an ideal position to become a major industrial centre.

The two railway companies amalgamated in 1850 to form the Glasgow & South Western Railway, which dominated rail services in Ayrshire but faced competition for access to Kilmarnock from the large Glasgow-based Caledonian Railway. Using a subsidiary company, the 'Caley' promoted a line from the city to Barrhead and Neilston, sparking heated arguments and hard bargaining before the two companies agreed to extend and operate it as a joint line. This more direct route opened in 1878, and at the same time the old station house, built in 1850, was superseded by a new station building. In 1923 the two rival companies became part of the London, Midland & Scottish Railway (LMS), which was taken into public ownership when the railways were nationalised in 1948.

The Glasgow & South Western Railway built workshops on a 13-acre site to the south of the tracks and west of the station. These opened in 1856 and between then and 1921 the company built 392 locomotives there. The LMS used the facility for repair work, but this ceased four years after nationalisation and in 1959 the works were finally closed. This old locomotive, thought to have been built in Glasgow for the Caledonian Railway, is seen beside the machine shop in 1945.

With two big railway companies serving the town, goods handling and train servicing facilities were duplicated. The Caledonian Railway had a yard on the north side of the tracks, seen here in 1937 some years after it had become the property of the LMS. Its run-down appearance suggests it was surplus to requirements. The houses on the left were in Henrietta Street. Nazareth House, in Hill Street, is on the extreme right.

A number of industries grew up to supply equipment to Kilmarnock's coal mines, one of which, begun by a young engineer named Andrew Barclay, became nationally important. There were two related strands to the business, mining equipment and industrial steam locomotives, both of which feature in this advertisement from a 1908 mining exhibition catalogue.

Andrew Barclay started his business in Portland Street in 1840. After seven years he moved to a larger site in West Langlands Street, at which point he experienced the first of several financial crises when money expected from the sale of a patent was never paid. Despite this, with larger premises he could take on more and bigger projects. To complete these he had castings made at the Caledonian Foundry in Glasgow (there was no suitable local foundry), naming his own workshop 'Caledonia Works' after this connection.

In the 1870s bankruptcy followed the purchase of an almost worthless mine in Devon and a failed attempt to establish a Cumbrian ironworks. Despite this, Andrew Barclay's creditors kept the business afloat, trusting in his skills as an engineer to salvage their investment. He did, but for the next two decades the company was rarely financially secure as 'old Barclay' resisted attempts to restructure it on a sound financial footing. His sideline of making telescopes (he was a keen astronomer) further irked his backers. In 1894 he was finally ousted from control, allowing the company to trade on the Barclay name for engineering excellence and grow in strength.

The company survived the Depression of the 1920s and emerged from the Second World War well equipped to meet future challenges. The nationalisation of Britain's railways and mines substantially reduced its customers, but Barclay's diversified into the production of diesel locomotives and sought out export markets, while also continuing to supply steam locomotives. It became part of the Leeds-based Hunslett Group in August 1972, changing its name to Hunslett-Barclay in 1989. This picture shows a 'pug', as these little industrial steam locomotives were known.

In 1876, at the height of Andrew Barclay's financial troubles, a fire destroyed part of the Caledonia Works. Two employees – works manager Thomas Grant and foreman William Ritchie – thought this would finish the company and left to set up on their own in a former engineering shop at Townholm. Gossip in the town suggested that they took drawings with them, because Grant, Ritchie's pugs were very like those of Andrew Barclay's, as this picture shows. True or not, the firm became a major supplier of colliery locomotives and winding engines. One of the latter has been preserved at the Scottish Mining Museum, the Lady Victoria Colliery, Newtongrange, Midlothian. The company ceased trading in 1926.

Coal is the compressed remains of trees that once grew in primeval swamps: the swamp beds formed fireclay so the two minerals are often found together. At Southhook mine the six-foot Lady Ha' seam had a layer of coal on top of clay, and bricks were made from the latter. There was a separate fifteen-foot seam of clay which was used to make sanitary ware. With such extensive deposits, Kilmarnock became a centre for the fireclay industry and three companies predominated: Southhook Potteries, J. & M. Craig and J. & R. Howie. Works were located at Hurlford, Crosshouse and Dreghorn, but there were also some within the burgh boundary. Craig's operated a fireclay works at Hillhead from the 1850s to the 1930s, and also had a sanitary pottery at Longpark which was taken over in 1918 by Shanks of Barrhead, one of the industry's giants. In 1963 Shanks took over Southhook Potteries whose Bonnyton Works, opened in the 1880s, were closed a few years later. They are seen in these two photos while still operational. After taking over Howie's, Shanks formed the Howie-Southhook Company in 1966 and concentrated production at Hurlford and Longpark. By the 1980s fireclay production in the Kilmarnock area had ceased.

Pattern No. 506
HOTEL LAVATORY

Pattern No. 538
HAIRDRESSER'S LAVATORY

Pattern No. 541
SURGEON'S LAVATORY

Pattern No. 2502
HOSPITAL BEDPAN SINK

Pattern No. 1000
URINAL RANGE WITH GLASS
ANTI-SPLASH PLATES

Southhook Potteries Ltd.

MANUFACTURERS OF :—

GLAZED SANITARY FIRECLAY WARE

GLAZED BRICKS

GLAZED WALL TILES

FIRE BRICKS

INSULATING FIREBRICKS

BUILDING BRICKS

SEWAGE AND DRAIN PIPES

Bonnyton Works ... ...
... Kilmarnock, Scotland

Telegrams: " Southhook, Kilmarnock "
Telephone: No. 531 (Private Exchange)

This advertisement from 1933 shows the range of products made by Southhook Potteries.

This pit at Springside, thought to be Springhill No. 3, was typical of the small units associated with the fireclay industry. It was worked by J. & R. Howie of Hurlford. Coal was also won from what was known as the Wee seam.

The Coal Mines Act of 1911 was a far-reaching piece of legislation, designed – amongst other things – to improve working conditions and safety in the industry. One of its provisions required coal owners to establish rescue brigades. The Ayrshire owners set up a rescue station at Bonnyton in 1912, where men from individual collieries came to be trained. There were mock-ups of underground conditions, and recruits had to undergo strenuous physical tests and perform rigorous simulated rescues before they were accepted into a team. They had to do it all again during regular reassessments to show they were still up to the task. Only the fittest and finest became members of rescue brigades.

This picture, thought to date from the 1920s, shows Bonnyton Road looking west from its junction with Stevenson Street. The fine run of four-in-a-block houses on the left is Kilgour Terrace. Behind the knot of people in the distance is a shop used at the time by the Co-op.

Fullarton Street is seen here looking south from the junction with Bonnyton Road, with Inkerman Place on the right. This was an area once dominated by the sights, sounds and smoke of industry: the upper corner window of the small tenement block on the left would have had a view across the road to Brownlee's timber yard, the Britannia engineering works, and both the railway and its workshops. The picture was used as a postcard in 1908 by someone who helpfully wrote a '2' on the roof to indicate their house to the recipient of the card.

The imposing Prudential Chambers filled the gushet between Langlands Brae on the left and West George Street (right). In this mid-1930s picture, the George Cinema, opened in 1922, can be seen beyond the ornate Victorian-era Prudential building. The cinema could seat 750 people in the stalls and 450 on the balcony. One Sunday in 1940 a fire broke out between the cinema floor and the ceilings of the shops below, but the mess was cleared up quickly and Monday's show went on with a barricade around the damaged floor. The George became a bingo hall in 1961.

The railway transformed Kilmarnock in many ways, although the most obvious physical change was the imposing viaduct running across the northern edge of the town centre. The arch across the top end of Portland Street is seen here with the building housing the appropriately named Bridge Bar crammed up against it – space was never wasted in an old Scots town.

The arch also dominates this picture of Portland Street, with the George Hotel on the left. Kilmarnock is not known for its hotels; indeed for a time it was notable for how few it had, people preferring, presumably, to seek accommodation in Glasgow or by the seaside at Troon or Ayr. The George was an exception. Built as a coaching inn in the early nineteenth century, it had a large hall which hosted a variety of functions, including meetings of the town's Burns Club which were held there from the 1840s. The hotel closed in 1920. The top of the High United Free Church tower can be seen above the viaduct parapet.

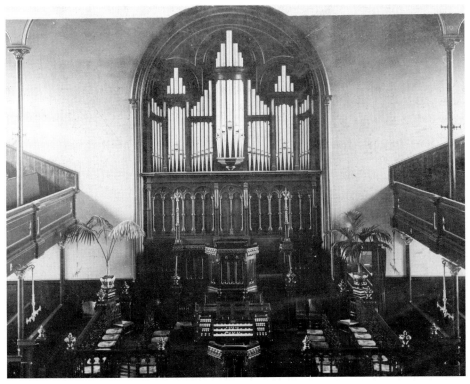

The number of church buildings in Scotland increased dramatically after 1843, when large numbers of ministers and their congregations left the Established Church of Scotland and formed the Free Church following an event known as the Disruption. In Kilmarnock the minister of the High Church, with most of his congregation and many members of the Laigh Kirk, set up a new Free High Church. Until a new church was built in 1844 they worshipped in the King Street Relief Church. The damaging divisions began to heal in 1900 when the United Presbyterian Church (an amalgam of the secession churches) and the Free Church came together as the United Free Church. In 1923 the UF Church reunited with the Church of Scotland and Kilmarnock's High UF Church (illustrated here) became the West High Church.

Sitting high above Wellington Street, Kilmarnock Infirmary was built to the designs of local architect William Railton and opened in 1868. The scale and confidence of the building says much about the civic pride of Kilmarnock folk in those pre-National Health Service days, when such institutions were paid for out of public subscriptions and local funds. Despite the subsequent addition of other buildings, it was realised as early as the 1930s that a larger hospital was needed, but the infirmary remained in use until Crosshouse Hospital was opened in 1982. Gutted by fire in the 1990s, the original building was subsequently demolished and the site used for housing.

The first Catholic church in Kilmarnock since the Reformation of 1560 was built in 1847 following the removal of legal restrictions on Catholic forms of worship. At the time the town had a sizeable Catholic population which was growing as workers, mainly from Ireland, were attracted by the growth of industry. As well as catering for people's spiritual needs, the church also sought to deal with social problems, erecting the imposing Nazareth House in Hill Street in 1890. The Poor Sisters of Nazareth used it to provide a home for orphaned children and elderly, homeless men.

Running north from the Cross, Fore Street and Soulis Street led to High Street, seen here from the railway viaduct. In the left foreground, at the northern end of Soulis Street, is the graveyard of the High Church. High Street Public School is in the left background. To the right are the chimneys of Bishopfield and Townhead Woollen Mills, the latter situated off Menford Lane. Dean Lane branched off towards Beansburn at the northern end of High Street, while the main line of the street continued across Townhead Bridge to Townholm. Iron, engineering and textile industries lined the east bank of the river there. The lie of the land, the bends in the river and the flow of water were all factors in the siting of these early industries.

This view from the high ground of Kay Park shows the area between High Street and the river. It was a warren of activity, crammed with houses, shops and a variety of small workshops. Mills used the water for power and lined the riverside. Wholesale redevelopment has meant that the only identifiable structures that remain are the railway viaduct and High Church, both on the left.

Before moving to Portland Street in 1923, the Scottish General Transport Company operated from the old butter market in Green Street. This was Kilmarnock's first bus station and was also used by Dick Brothers, whose garage came to occupy a large site off Green Street. Their name can just be made out, painted on the door above the word 'Garage'. The same premises were used by the Corporation buses during the period they overlapped with the trams (which operated from the depot at Riccarton Bridge). So when the bus station moved to Green Street in the late 1970s, it was in a sense just coming home.

Green Street, seen here about 1900 looking north from Waterloo Street, took its name from the old town green. The prominent three-storey building to the right of centre was at the junction with Duke Street. Nothing now remains of the old street, which became part of the ring road system in the 1970s. The new Green Street Bridge opened in 1975.

Clark Street, named after the one-time owner of Elmbank House, was one link in a chain of streets running round the base of Elmbank. This postcard view was sent to Australia in 1911. The message on the back is a fascinating, if unflattering, social comment on the town at that time: 'The four children on the right seem to be very poor. They look as if they were out begging. We have lots of these about our town.'

Robertson Place was erected by and for members of the Kilmarnock Building Company. This co-operative venture was formed in 1824, and members had to pay an entry fee and monthly subscription until the costs of the building work were covered. No other housing appears to have been built in the town this way, and after completion the members of the original scheme seem to have been on their own, with Robertson Place suffering from a lack of maintenance. It is seen here at its south-eastern end in the early twentieth century, with the little grocery shop on the left doubling as the Welbeck Street post office. At the extreme right-hand edge of the picture is John Ferguson's Bridge Inn.

These two pictures were taken at the same time. The one on the right shows the Kilmarnock Water looking north from Green Street Bridge, with a mill and footbridge framed by an arch of the railway viaduct in the distance. Two men appear to be fishing and have attracted a small group of onlookers, who have paused for a moment to face the camera as the photographer frames a shot of London Road looking back towards Duke Street.

On the left is the Corn Exchange building, with its prominent Albert Tower. Erected to the designs of James Ingram in 1862/63, the building was extended by his son Robert in 1886. When its original role as a market hall faded, it became a variety theatre, and was the first venue in the town to screen films, either interspersed with variety acts or on alternate nights. Films eventually took over completely and it was named the Palace Picture House. This closed in 1949, but in 1951 the venue became a 625-seat civic theatre, the Exchange Theatre, opening with a show called *Kilmarnock Merry-go-round*. It closed again in 1954, before reopening and stuttering along until a fire in 1979 forced another closure. After restoration it opened as the Palace Theatre in 1982 with a show starring Johnnie Beattie.

The small mansion house of Braehead was built about 1765 for William Paterson, a close friend of Robert Burns. It sat off London Road, screened by trees, and having been somewhat altered over the years was demolished in 1965. The Braehead Court housing development has since been built on the site.

Kilmarnock Bowling Club is seen here cradled by the path leading into Kay Park. The club was founded in 1740, and although it occupied a couple of other greens before moving to its present location in 1867 it is crucially still in existence, thereby maintaining its claim to be the oldest bowls club in the country. The building poking into the left-hand edge of the picture is the Henderson Church, built to the designs of Thomas Smellie in 1907. Also on the left, in the background above the railway viaduct, is the distinctive spire of the High Church.

People travelling along London Road originally had to go up and over a steep bank at Braehead, and in the 1820s unemployed men were given the job of cutting through the bank to reduce the gradient. The remnant of the old road can be seen here, forming a ramp to Braeside Street. The railings in the foreground sit on top of the cutting's retaining wall. Robert Burns' great friend Tam Samson lived in the house on the left, which according to the sign on this postcard, published about 1905 by Tommy Rodger, was still being used by his descendants to carry on the family seedsman's business.

Kilmarnock Academy originated as the burgh school in the seventeenth century and gained a reputation for excellence, despite having to compete with other schools for pupils. The rivalry ended when the 1872 Education Act came into force, and with it a school board charged with ensuring that every child aged between five and thirteen went to school. During its early years the academy occupied a number of premises around the town before moving into this purpose-built school at the top of Braeside Street in 1898. Designed by the architect Robert Ingram, it is still used by the school, along with later additions and extensions.

Kilmarnock Technical School, the forerunner of Kilmarnock College, was built in 1909 as part of Kilmarnock Academy. It is seen here from Elmbank Drive in the 1930s, with the grounds of the Dick Institute on the right. Also on the right is a wee boy with a cart made out of a wooden box and old pram wheels, with bits of wood for handles – the sort of crude, home-made, hazard-filled improvisation that was infinitely more fun than shop-bought plastic perfection. The only other vehicle, a laundry van, sits where cars compete for parking spaces today.

War memorials were erected by communities across the country when it became clear that the bodies of men killed during the First World War would not be brought home for burial. Kilmarnock's memorial was designed by James Millar in the form of a small Greek temple. Inside over 850 names are displayed on bronze tablets, complemented by a bronze figure of Victory, gifted to the community by the sculptor David McGill. The unveiling ceremony, performed in May 1927 by Air Marshall Sir H.M. Trenchard, was accompanied by a service of praise in which the Kilmarnock Musical Club Choir and the burgh band took part. The guard of honour was made up of the Ayrshire Imperial Yeomanry, the Royal Scots Fusiliers and Royal Field Artillery. Also on parade were a number of ex-servicemen, the Kilmarnock Cadet Corps and the local Voluntary Aid Detachment.

Across the road from the war memorial is the Dick Institute. This was established as a museum, art gallery and library to accommodate an internationally famous geological collection which was bequeathed to the town by James Thomson FGS. A home for the collection was initially found in Elmbank House, but when it outgrew the available space Provost David Mackay enlisted the help of a former son of Kilmarnock, James Dick, to find an alternative. He had made his money in industry and mining, and agreed to fund a new building named after his brother, Robert. The old house was demolished and the Dick Institute opened in April 1901. Disaster struck in November 1909 when a fire, thought to have been caused by an electrical fault, destroyed the building and most of the collections – including the original geological bequest.

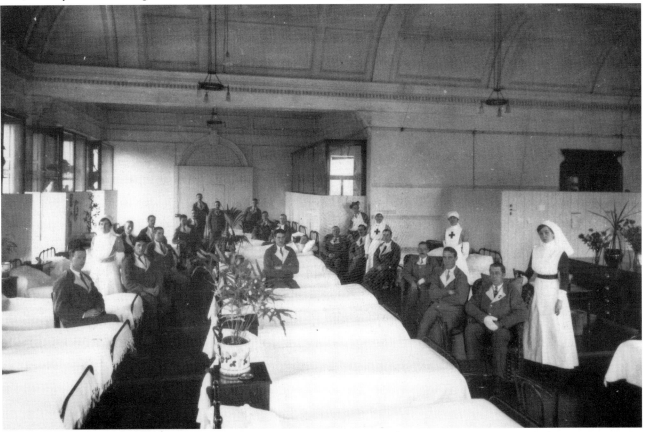

Some artefacts were salvaged from the ruins, new ones were donated and the Dick Institute was rebuilt, but in May 1917 it was taken over as a wartime emergency Red Cross hospital – the largest in Ayrshire. This picture shows one of the galleries fitted out as a ward for wounded servicemen. Thankfully, the 'Dick' has survived those trying early years to become one of the country's best known and most respected institutions.

This corner of London Road and Elmbank Avenue was a busy place in the 1920s, with the war memorial erected in 1927 and the Masonic Hall (on the right) built in 1926. In front of the hall is the marble statue of Jimmie Shaw which was moved here from the Cross in 1929. The site must have seemed ideal at the time, but the lone statue now looks a bit isolated. The academy building can be seen in the distance, while half-hidden by trees on the left are the war memorial and technical college.

This view from 1950 shows London Road looking back towards the Henderson Church, with some of the fine Victorian villas that characterise the road on the right.

These two pictures of London Road looking towards the town were taken close to the junction with Glebe Road in the years before the First World War. They show the road as it was, with tracks and cable stanchions for the tram service to and from Hurlford. This ceased in December 1924, eighteen months before the closure of the main part of the system.

At the start of the twentieth century, housing for working people was provided by private landlords or large industrial concerns. Conditions were often squalid, and although local authorities had powers to effect improvements these were rarely used. A Royal Commission was set up in 1912 to look into the problem and presented its findings five years later. The Commission's shocking conclusions resulted in the 1919 Housing Act, which fundamentally changed the way society provided housing. Subsequent Acts followed, all giving local authorities the power to clear substandard property and build decent homes for rent. In Kilmarnock a number of schemes were developed, including this one off London Road. It is seen here under construction in the 1920s, looking towards Culzean Crescent from Holehouse Road, with Alloway Avenue and Piersland Park on the right.

The 31-acre Kay Park was donated to the town by insurance broker Alexander Kay and opened in 1879. It was, as the picture shows, furnished with those must-haves of the well-appointed Victorian park, a bandstand and an ornate fountain. It also had a fine view of the Townhead and Bishopfield Woollen Works across the river.

If this small crowd of people is anything to go by, the bandstand and fountain were popular focal points in the park. Perhaps its biggest attraction, however, was the memorial to Robert Burns, which is in the background. Kay Park was also graced by the Reformers' Monument, out of view to the left. This was erected in 1885 to mark the occasion, in 1816, when almost half the town's population gathered to support demands for parliamentary reform. Two men, Captain Thomas Baird and Alexander McLaren, were arrested, fined and sent to prison for six months for their part in the protest. All they wanted was a vote – something we often take for granted these days.

When the proposal to erect a statue of Robert Burns was put to a meeting in the George Hotel in 1877 it was greeted with such enthusiasm that the organising committee soon found itself with enough money to ask architect Robert S. Ingram to design something bigger. He proposed an ornate, two-storey building of red Ballochmyle stone, serving both as a frame for the statue and a museum. A competition to design the statue was won by Edinburgh sculptor W. Grant Stevenson, who created the eight-foot likeness from Sicilian marble. The completed monument was unveiled in front of a huge crowd in August 1879.

The museum contained a wide range of Burnsian artefacts, including a number of portraits, copies of his published works, a model of his cottage … and his frying pan. There were also objects of general interest, including relics from the crannog of Lochlee, a small portion of Atlantic cable, and a stuffed kangaroo from Australia. Succeeding generations didn't fully share the Victorians' enthusiasm for such things, and the monument became a target for vandals. Elements of the partially demolished structure have been saved as the centrepiece of a new Burns centre.

This picture, looking south from Beansburn to Dean Street, shows the north of the town during a period of change. Tramlines are no longer in evidence, but although the picture is thought to date from the mid-1930s the poles that carried the electric wires are still in place, and apparently being used as street lighting standards. The junction with Campbeltown Drive, formerly Hillhead Avenue, is on the right. Dean Park is on the left.

The houses on the right of the upper picture are seen here above the steep terraced slope of Dean Park, at the foot of which flows the Beans – or Beanies – Burn. This gave its name to the village, which was absorbed into Kilmarnock in 1871 when the town's boundaries were extended. The park was unofficially known as the 'Toll Park' because an old tollhouse was sited just above the slope in the days when the Glasgow Road operated as a toll, or turnpike, road.

The Beansburn tram terminus was located where the road to Knockinlaw Farm joined the Glasgow Road. The tram service no doubt hastened the development of nearby farmland for housing, and Knockinlaw Road is seen here in the mid-1930s when new. Just poking into the picture on the left is the gable of an older building known as Dean House. A bus stop in front of it, on the main road, perpetuates the location of the original tram terminus.

The entrance to Castle Drive is on the left of this 1930s view looking north along the Glasgow Road. The drive's crescent-shaped layout presumably allowed buses to turn more easily at what was then the northern limit of the town. The houses on the far left are in Rowallan Drive.

Before Harriet Bridge was built people used the nearby ford to cross the river. The Kilmarnock Iron Foundry was just to the left of here, and had the photographer regarded it as sufficiently picturesque to include he would also have taken in the confluence of the Kilmarnock Water and the Beans Burn, along with the ford just upstream. The houses of Gillsburn Place are in the background.

Lauder Bridge spanned the Kilmarnock Water below Dean Castle. Its name reflected the efforts of Hugh Lauder, proprietor of Lauder's Emporium in King Street, to raise funds for its construction. In accepting the bridge on behalf of Kilmarnock Corporation in early June 1905, Provost Hood expressed the hope that 'people of good will' would see to it that 'it was neither harmed nor injured in any way'. His words were prophetic, because no sooner had Mrs Lauder formally opened the bridge than people crowded on to it in such numbers that a connecting link to one of the suspension cables snapped, and the 90-foot bridge deck fell into the shallow river, injuring eight people. The Lauder Bridge was subsequently repaired, and in more recent years has been superseded by Dean Road.

The summer-clad women and girls in this picture are standing on a 'rustic' bridge over the Beans Burn with Dean Park spread out behind them.

Dean Park came into existence in 1906 when the proprietor of the Dean Estate, Lord Howard de Walden, gifted about six acres of ground between Glasgow Road and the Kilmarnock Water to the town. In a letter to the council he wrote about the distance that the Kay and Howard Parks were from the north of the town, which also needed a recreation ground. He was insistent that the park should be for children and 'not for football, cricket, hockey, cycle or path racing, or any game or sports for grown-up people'. He imposed conditions on the layout and fencing, and insisted on the widening of the Glasgow Road, for which he also donated land. The council accepted his offer and Dean Park was opened in 1907, undergoing subsequent enlargement. The middle picture shows the area close to the Beans Burn in 1924, with the house known as Deanhill in the right background. The lower view is of the same section of park about ten years later.

Dean Castle sits to the north of the town beside the Fenwick or Borland Water, although it is hard to see the defensive merits of the site as the stream would be unlikely to deter a determined attacker. The oldest surviving buildings, contained within a walled courtyard, date from the early and mid fifteenth century when the castle and lands were in the possession of the Boyd family. They forfeited the estate in 1469 when found guilty of treason, but it was returned to them in 1545. Following a fire in 1735 the family went to live in Kilmarnock House and the old castle fell into disrepair.

In 1899 the castle and estate were inherited by the 8th Lord Howard de Walden, Thomas Evelyn Scott-Ellis. He set about having the keep, tower and palace restored, and the work was completed in 1946, the same year that he died. Thirty years later his son, the 9th Earl, gifted the castle – along with its collection of arms, armour, tapestries and musical instruments – to Kilmarnock & Loudoun District Council. Forty acres of ground were also included in the gift and an additional 160 acres were purchased by the district council, which opened it as a country park in 1980. The castle is seen here before restoration with some horticultural additions in the form of greenhouses and cold frames.

Dean Castle's so-called dower house was a small country house that dated mostly from the nineteenth century, by which time the main castle was derelict and uninhabitable. It was used as a visitor centre for a while, and has since been restored as a conference and function venue.

Many of the buildings in Kilmarnock's main streets were built with stone from Dean Quarry. It was worked for freestone – stone that could be cut and worked in any direction – for most of the nineteenth century, closing in 1872. In the early years stone was taken from either side of the Borland Water, an inconvenience that was solved by diverting the flow away from the quarry. The operators, J. & M. Craig, also won coal and fireclay from a shallow pit situated within the quarry, operating a small brickworks alongside it. When the workings were abandoned they filled up with water, leaving Dean Quarry House with a larger than usual garden pond.

Assloss House, to the north of Dean Castle, was the home of William Parker, one of Burns' early patrons and founder of the Kilmarnock Bank. His banking exploits were not wholly successful, and he had to dispose of lands at Barleith, and elsewhere, to pay for losses. He nevertheless managed to hang on to Assloss and it remained in the Parker family for some time after his death.

This picture of Andrew Montgomery ploughing with a splendid pair of heavy horses was taken on Assloss Farm.

Despite being replete with all the battlemented pretence of an ancient stronghold, Craufurdland Castle is of no great antiquity, although it does incorporate a late sixteenth-century tower house. According to local legend it is linked to Dean Castle, just over a mile away to the south-west, by a long lost underground passage. Such passages crop up in stories all over Scotland and are more likely to be based on fertile imagination than hard fact!